Mastering Your Taxes

A Comprehensive Guide to Successful Tax Preparation

Cheryl Waller, MBA

ISBN: 9798396637870

LEGAL DISCLAIMER: This publication is designed to provide accurate and authoritative information in regard to the subject matter covered. The publisher is not engaged in rendering legal, accounting, or other professional services. If legal advice or other expert assistance is required, the services of a competent professional should be sought.

TABLE OF CONTENTS

THE BASICS: UNDERSTANDING TAXATION AND YOUR RESPONSIBILITIES

Taxation is an integral part of our society, playing a crucial role in funding public services, infrastructure, and government operations. Understanding taxation and your responsibilities as a taxpayer is essential to ensure compliance with the law and to optimize your financial situation. In this chapter, we will delve into the fundamentals of taxation, shedding light on key concepts, types of taxes, and the obligations that come with them.

What is Taxation?

Taxation is the process by which governments collect money from individuals and businesses to finance public expenditures. These funds are utilized to support a wide range of services, including healthcare, education, defense, transportation, and social welfare programs. Taxes are levied by various levels of government, such as federal, state, and local authorities, depending on the jurisdiction.

Why Do We Pay Taxes?

Taxes serve multiple purposes within a society. They provide the necessary funds to maintain public infrastructure, such as roads, bridges, and public transportation systems. Taxes also support public services like schools, hospitals, police, and fire departments. Furthermore, taxes are utilized to address social and economic disparities through welfare programs and income redistribution initiatives.

Types of Taxes:

There are various types of taxes that individuals and businesses encounter. Here are some common categories:

Income Taxes:

Income taxes are levied on the earnings of individuals and businesses. They are typically calculated based on the amount of income earned within a specific period. Income tax rates can vary based on income levels, with progressive tax systems imposing higher rates on higher income brackets.

Sales Taxes:

Sales taxes are imposed on the purchase of goods and services. They are usually calculated as a percentage of the sale price and can be levied at the federal, state, or local levels. Sales tax rates and the items subject to taxation can differ across jurisdictions.

Property Taxes:

Property taxes are assessed on the value of real estate properties owned by individuals and businesses. These taxes are typically used to fund local government services, such as schools and infrastructure maintenance.

Payroll Taxes:

Payroll taxes are deducted from employees' wages and are used to fund social security, Medicare, and other social insurance programs. Employers are also responsible for contributing to these taxes on behalf of their employees.

Excise Taxes:

Excise taxes are imposed on specific goods or activities, such as alcohol, tobacco, gasoline, and luxury items. These taxes are often levied to discourage consumption or to fund specific programs related to the taxed items.

Tax Obligations:

As a taxpayer, you have certain responsibilities and obligations to fulfill. Understanding these responsibilities is crucial to ensure compliance and avoid potential penalties. Here are some key tax obligations:

Filing Tax Returns:

One of the primary obligations of taxpayers is to file their tax returns accurately and timely. Tax returns provide a comprehensive summary of your income, deductions, and credits for a specific tax year. The filing deadline can vary depending on the jurisdiction and the type of taxpayer.

Reporting Income:

It is essential to report all sources of income accurately. This includes wages, self-employment income, rental income, investment income, and any other income-generating activities. Failure to report income can lead to penalties and legal consequences.

Keeping Records:

Maintaining proper records and documentation of your financial transactions is crucial for tax purposes. This includes receipts, invoices, bank statements, and other relevant documents. These records serve as evidence to support the accuracy of your tax return and can be essential in case of an audit or dispute.

Paying Taxes:

Meeting your tax obligations also entails paying the required amount of taxes owed. This can be done through various methods, such as payroll deductions, estimated tax payments, or regular installments. Failing to pay taxes on time can result in penalties and interest charges.

Understanding Deductions and Credits:

As a taxpayer, you have the opportunity to reduce your tax liability through deductions and credits. Deductions lower your taxable income, while credits provide a dollar-for-dollar reduction in the amount of tax owed. Understanding the available deductions and credits can help you optimize your tax situation and potentially increase your tax refund.

Compliance with Tax Laws:

Tax laws can be complex and subject to changes and updates. It is essential to stay informed about the applicable tax laws and regulations to ensure compliance. This can involve researching tax publications, consulting tax professionals, or utilizing online resources provided by tax authorities.

Understanding taxation and your responsibilities as a taxpayer is the foundation for successful tax preparation. By comprehending the basics of taxation, including types of taxes, obligations, and compliance, you can navigate the tax landscape with confidence. This knowledge empowers you to optimize your financial situation, fulfill your tax obligations, and avoid potential penalties. In the following chapters, we will delve deeper into specific aspects of tax preparation, equipping you with the tools and strategies necessary for successful tax management.

NAVIGATING THE TAX LANDSCAPE: LATEST LAWS, UPDATES, AND CHANGES

The tax landscape is dynamic and constantly evolving, with new laws, updates, and changes introduced regularly. Staying informed about these developments is essential for taxpayers to ensure compliance and optimize their tax planning strategies. In this chapter, we will explore how to navigate the ever-changing tax landscape, understand the importance of staying updated, and discuss key resources to help you stay informed about the latest tax laws.

The Importance of Staying Updated:

Tax laws undergo revisions and updates for various reasons, such as economic changes, policy shifts, or administrative requirements. Staying updated with the latest tax laws is crucial for several reasons:

Compliance:

Tax laws dictate your rights and obligations as a taxpayer. By staying updated, you can ensure compliance with the law and avoid penalties or legal issues that may arise due to ignorance of tax regulations.

Tax Planning:

Changes in tax laws can present opportunities for tax planning and optimization. By understanding the new rules, you can structure your finances and transactions in a way that minimizes your tax liability and maximizes your tax benefits.

Maximizing Deductions and Credits:

Tax laws often introduce new deductions, credits, or changes to existing ones. Staying updated allows you to take advantage of these opportunities and ensure you claim all eligible deductions and credits, potentially reducing your overall tax burden.

Avoiding Surprises:

By staying informed about tax law changes, you can avoid unpleasant surprises during the tax preparation process. Being aware of new requirements or limitations can help you plan ahead and gather the necessary documentation or adjust your financial strategies accordingly.

Sources of Tax Law Updates:

To navigate the tax landscape effectively, you need reliable sources of information that provide timely updates on tax laws. Here are some key sources to consider:

Government Tax Websites:

Government tax websites at the federal, state, and local levels are valuable sources of information for tax law updates. These websites often provide official publications, forms, instructions, and announcements regarding tax law changes. Examples include the Internal Revenue Service (IRS) website in the United States or the HM Revenue & Customs (HMRC) website in the United Kingdom.

Tax News Publications:

Tax news publications, whether in print or online, specialize in reporting and analyzing tax-related developments. Subscribing to reputable tax publications can keep you informed about the latest tax laws, court decisions, and regulatory updates. Examples include Tax Notes, Tax Analysts, or reputable financial news outlets that cover tax-related topics.

Professional Tax Organizations:

Professional tax organizations, such as tax associations or accounting bodies, often provide members with access to tax updates and resources. These organizations may offer newsletters, webinars, or conferences that cover the latest tax developments. Joining these organizations can be beneficial for professionals or individuals seeking more in-depth tax information.

Tax Advisors and Professionals:

Consulting with tax advisors, accountants, or tax professionals can provide personalized guidance and updates on tax laws. These professionals stay abreast of tax developments and can help you understand the implications of changes specific to your financial situation. They can also assist in tax planning, compliance, and identifying opportunities for optimization.

Online Government Resources:

Many tax authorities provide online resources, including databases, guides, FAQs, and e-learning platforms. These resources can help taxpayers understand tax laws, access forms and publications, and stay updated on changes. Examples include the IRS Taxpayer Advocate Service or the Australian Taxation Office (ATO) website.

Adapting to Tax Law Changes:

When tax laws change, it is crucial to adapt your tax planning and preparation strategies accordingly. Here are some steps to navigate changes effectively:

Review and Understand Changes:

Carefully review and understand the changes in tax laws relevant to your situation. Consider how they impact your income, deductions, credits, or specific transactions.

Consult with Professionals:

Engage with tax advisors or professionals to assess the impact of the changes on your tax situation. They can provide guidance on adjusting your tax planning strategies or taking advantage of new opportunities.

Update Record-Keeping Systems:

Adapt your record-keeping systems to ensure you capture the necessary information and documentation required by the new tax laws. This includes maintaining records of income, expenses, and supporting documents to substantiate your tax positions.

Plan and Adjust Finances:

Explore tax planning opportunities provided by the changes in tax laws. For example, changes to deductions or credits may require adjusting your financial strategies to optimize tax benefits.

Stay Informed:

Continue to monitor tax law developments even after adapting to specific changes. The tax landscape remains dynamic, and future updates may impact your tax situation or present new planning opportunities.

Navigating the tax landscape requires staying informed about the latest tax laws, updates, and changes. By understanding the importance of staying updated, accessing reliable sources of information, and adapting to tax law changes, you can ensure compliance, optimize your tax planning strategies, and avoid surprises during the tax preparation process. In the next chapter, we will delve into the fundamentals of tax forms and schedules, providing insights into how to navigate these documents effectively.

DECODING TAX FORMS: A COMPREHENSIVE OVERVIEW

Tax forms are an integral part of the tax preparation process, serving as the framework for reporting income, claiming deductions and credits, and calculating tax liability. However, tax forms can be complex and overwhelming for many taxpayers. In this chapter, we will provide a comprehensive overview of tax forms, explaining their purpose, common components, and how to navigate them effectively.

Understanding the Purpose of Tax Forms:

Tax forms are standardized documents used by taxpayers to report their financial information to tax authorities. These forms serve multiple purposes:

Income Reporting:

Tax forms require taxpayers to report their income from various sources, such as wages, self-employment, investments, rental properties, and other taxable activities.

Deduction and Credit Reporting:

Tax forms allow taxpayers to claim deductions and credits they are eligible for, reducing their taxable income or tax liability.

Tax Calculation:

By providing relevant financial information, tax forms facilitate the calculation of tax liability or tax refund owed to or by the taxpayer.

Compliance Monitoring:

Tax forms enable tax authorities to monitor compliance, identify discrepancies, and conduct audits if necessary.

Common Components of Tax Forms:

While tax forms can vary based on the jurisdiction and individual circumstances, there are common components found in most tax forms:

Personal Information:

Tax forms typically require taxpayers to provide their personal information, including their name, address, Social Security Number (SSN), or Taxpayer Identification Number (TIN).

Filing Status:

Tax forms require taxpayers to indicate their filing status, such as Single, Married Filing Jointly, Married Filing Separately, Head of Household, or Qualifying Widow(er) with Dependent Child. Filing status determines tax rates and eligibility for certain deductions or credits.

Income Reporting:

Tax forms have sections for reporting different types of income, such as wages, salaries, dividends, interest, capital gains, rental income, and self-employment income. Each income source may have specific lines or schedules dedicated to it.

Deductions and Credits:

Tax forms include sections for claiming deductions and credits. Deductions reduce taxable income, while credits provide a direct reduction in tax liability. Common deductions and credits include those for education expenses, mortgage interest, child tax credit, and earned income credit.

Tax Calculation:

Tax forms contain tables, schedules, or formulas for calculating tax liability based on the reported income, deductions, and credits. These calculations consider the applicable tax rates, exemptions, and tax brackets.

Signature and Date:

Tax forms require the taxpayer's signature and date of filing, certifying the accuracy of the information provided.

Navigating Tax Forms Effectively:

Navigating tax forms can be intimidating, but with a systematic approach, it becomes more manageable. Here are some tips to help you navigate tax forms effectively:

Read Instructions:

Start by carefully reading the instructions provided with the tax form. The instructions offer valuable guidance on completing the form correctly, understanding specific sections, and addressing common questions.

Gather Required Documents:

Before filling out the tax form, gather all the necessary documents, such as W-2 forms, 1099 forms, investment statements, and receipts for deductions or credits. Organize these documents according to the sections of the form to ensure accuracy and completeness.

Utilize Supporting Schedules and Worksheets:

Tax forms often include supporting schedules or worksheets for certain sections or specific deductions and credits. Use these additional forms to provide more detailed information or calculate specific amounts accurately.

Use Electronic Filing Options:

Consider utilizing electronic filing options, such as e-file or tax software, which can streamline the tax preparation process. Electronic filing helps reduce errors, perform automatic calculations, and receive faster confirmation of filing.

Seek Professional Assistance:

If you find tax forms overwhelming or have complex tax situations, consider seeking professional assistance from tax advisors or qualified tax professionals. They can guide you through the process, ensure accuracy, and help you optimize your tax situation.

Understanding tax forms is crucial for effective tax preparation. By comprehending their purpose, common components, and utilizing appropriate strategies, you can navigate tax forms with confidence. Reading instructions, gathering required documents, utilizing supporting schedules, and seeking professional assistance when needed are key steps to ensure accuracy and compliance. In the next chapter, we will delve into the importance of organizing your financial documents effectively, a crucial aspect of successful tax preparation.

DEMYSTIFYING TAX SCHEDULES: WHAT YOU NEED TO KNOW

Tax schedules are an integral part of the tax preparation process, providing detailed instructions and calculations for specific aspects of your tax return. While tax forms capture the broad overview of your financial information, tax schedules delve into specific areas such as business income, capital gains, or itemized deductions. In this chapter, we will demystify tax schedules, explaining their purpose, common types, and how to navigate them effectively.

Understanding the Purpose of Tax Schedules:

Tax schedules serve several purposes in the tax preparation process:

Detailed Reporting:

Tax schedules provide a platform to report specific types of income, deductions, or credits that require more detailed information than what can be captured on the main tax form.

Complex Calculations:

Certain tax calculations, such as determining taxable business income or calculating capital gains and losses, require additional computations. Tax schedules provide the framework for these calculations.

Supporting Documentation:

Tax schedules often require supporting documentation, such as receipts or statements, to substantiate the amounts reported or claimed.

Common Types of Tax Schedules:

While the specific tax schedules you encounter depend on your individual circumstances, there are several common types:

Schedule A: Itemized Deductions:

Schedule A is used to report itemized deductions, such as medical expenses, state and local taxes, mortgage interest, charitable contributions, and certain miscellaneous deductions.

Schedule B: Interest and Ordinary Dividends:

Schedule B is used to report interest income and ordinary dividends received during the tax year. It provides a breakdown of different sources of interest and dividends, such as bank accounts, bonds, or mutual funds.

Schedule C: Profit or Loss from Business:

Schedule C is used by self-employed individuals or sole proprietors to report business income or loss. It allows for the detailed reporting of business expenses, revenue, and deductions related to the operation of a business.

Schedule D: Capital Gains and Losses:

Schedule D is used to report capital gains and losses from the sale of assets, such as stocks, bonds, real estate, or other investments. It calculates the net gain or loss and determines the tax liability or deductible loss.

Schedule E: Supplemental Income and Loss:

Schedule E is used to report supplemental income or loss from rental properties, partnerships, S corporations, estates, trusts, or royalties. It provides a breakdown of income, expenses, and deductions related to these activities.

Schedule SE: Self-Employment Tax:

Schedule SE is used to calculate and report self-employment tax for individuals who have self-employment income. It determines the amount of Social Security and Medicare taxes owed by self-employed individuals.

Navigating Tax Schedules Effectively:

Navigating tax schedules can seem daunting, but with a systematic approach, it becomes more manageable. Here are some tips to help you navigate tax schedules effectively:

Determine the Relevant Schedules:

Identify the tax schedules that are applicable to your specific tax situation. This depends on the types of income, deductions, or credits you need to report.

Gather Supporting Documents:

Collect all the necessary supporting documents, such as receipts, statements, or financial records, required to complete the tax schedules accurately. Ensure that you have the necessary documentation to substantiate the amounts reported or claimed.

Read the Instructions:

Carefully read the instructions provided with each tax schedule. The instructions explain how to complete the schedule, which lines to fill out, and any specific calculations or requirements.

Use Worksheets and Examples:

Tax schedules often provide worksheets or examples to help you navigate complex calculations or determine specific amounts. Utilize these resources to ensure accuracy and understand the calculations required.

Seek Professional Assistance:

If you encounter challenges or have complex tax situations, consider seeking professional assistance from tax advisors or qualified tax professionals. They can guide you through the process, ensure accuracy, and provide expert advice on completing the tax schedules correctly.

Tax schedules play a crucial role in capturing detailed information and calculations for specific aspects of your tax return. Understanding their purpose, common types, and how to navigate them effectively is essential for accurate tax preparation. By identifying the relevant schedules, gathering supporting documents, reading instructions, using worksheets and examples, and seeking professional assistance when needed, you can navigate tax schedules with confidence. In the next chapter, we will delve into the

importance of organizing your financial documents
effectively, a crucial aspect of successful tax preparation.

ORGANIZING YOUR FINANCIAL DOCUMENTS: A STEP-BY-STEP APPROACH

Organizing your financial documents is a fundamental step in successful tax preparation. Keeping your financial records in order ensures accuracy, saves time, and helps you maximize deductions and credits while minimizing errors. In this chapter, we will provide a step-by-step approach to organizing your financial documents effectively, enabling smooth tax preparation and efficient retrieval of information when needed.

Assess Your Current Situation:

Begin by assessing your current financial document management system. Take an inventory of the documents you have and evaluate the organization methods you currently employ. This evaluation will help identify areas that need improvement and allow you to create a plan for organizing your financial documents effectively.

Determine the Necessary Documents:

Identify the types of financial documents you need to organize. This includes documents related to income, deductions, investments, expenses, and other financial transactions. Common financial documents include:

Income Documents:
Gather documents such as W-2 forms from employers, 1099 forms for freelance or contract work, and statements for interest or dividend income.

Deduction and Credit Documents:
Collect documents that support deductions and credits you plan to claim, such as receipts for charitable donations, mortgage interest statements, or education expense records.

Investment and Retirement Account Statements:
Compile statements for investment accounts, retirement accounts (e.g., 401(k) or IRA), and brokerage accounts.

Expense Receipts and Invoices:
Organize receipts and invoices for expenses that may be deductible, such as medical expenses, business-related expenses, or unreimbursed job-related expenses.

Property and Asset Records:
Keep records related to property ownership, including purchase/sale documents, mortgage statements, and

property tax records. Additionally, maintain records for other valuable assets like vehicles or collectibles.

Create a Document Storage System:

Establish a systematic document storage system that suits your needs and ensures easy access to necessary information. Consider the following steps:

Physical Filing System:

For physical documents, use a filing cabinet or file folders to categorize and store your financial documents. Create separate folders for different document types (e.g., income, deductions, investments) and label them clearly for easy identification.

Digital Filing System:

For digital documents, create folders on your computer or cloud storage platforms to organize and store electronic copies of your financial documents. Use clear and consistent file naming conventions to facilitate easy retrieval.

Subcategories and Labels:

Within each main category, create subcategories or labels to further categorize your documents. For example, within the "Deductions" category, create subcategories like "Charitable Donations," "Education Expenses," or "Medical Expenses" for better organization and quick reference.

Backup and Security:

Ensure you have a reliable backup system for your digital documents to protect against data loss. Consider using cloud storage or external hard drives for backup purposes. Additionally, implement appropriate security measures, such as strong passwords or encryption, to safeguard your financial information.

Establish a Document Retention Schedule:

Develop a document retention schedule that outlines how long you should keep different types of financial documents. This helps maintain an organized system while ensuring compliance with record-keeping requirements. Consult with tax professionals or legal experts for guidance on document retention periods, as they can vary based on jurisdiction and document type.

Regular Maintenance and Review:

To maintain an organized financial document system, establish a regular maintenance and review schedule. Set aside time each month or quarter to sort and file new documents, remove outdated or unnecessary ones, and ensure everything is in order. Regular review ensures your system stays up-to-date and facilitates efficient tax preparation.

Utilize Digital Tools:

Leverage digital tools and apps designed for document organization and management. Numerous software applications and mobile apps allow you to scan and store digital copies of your financial documents, easily categorize and tag them, set reminders for important deadlines, and access documents from anywhere.

Seek Professional Assistance:

If organizing your financial documents feels overwhelming, consider seeking professional assistance from a tax advisor or financial organizer. These professionals can provide guidance, offer organizational tips, and help you develop a system that suits your specific needs.

Organizing your financial documents is a crucial step in successful tax preparation. By assessing your current situation, determining the necessary documents, creating a document storage system, establishing a retention schedule, conducting regular maintenance and review, utilizing digital tools, and seeking professional assistance when needed, you can effectively manage your financial documents. An organized system saves time, reduces stress, and enables accurate and efficient tax preparation. In the next chapter, we will explore strategies for maximizing deductions and credits, optimizing your tax situation, and minimizing your tax liability.

MAXIMIZING DEDUCTIONS: STRATEGIES TO OPTIMIZE YOUR TAX SAVINGS

Maximizing deductions is a key strategy for optimizing your tax situation and reducing your overall tax liability. Deductions lower your taxable income, potentially resulting in significant tax savings. In this chapter, we will explore various strategies and tips to help you maximize your deductions effectively, ensuring you claim all eligible deductions and optimize your tax savings.

Understand the Difference Between Standard Deduction and Itemized Deductions:

Taxpayers have the option to choose between taking the standard deduction or itemizing deductions on their tax return. The standard deduction is a fixed amount that reduces your taxable income automatically. Itemized deductions, on the other hand, involve listing specific expenses you incurred during the tax year. Understanding the difference and choosing the approach that provides the most significant tax benefit is essential.

Identify Commonly Overlooked Deductions:

To maximize your deductions, it is crucial to be aware of commonly overlooked deductions. Some deductions that taxpayers may overlook include:

State Sales Tax Deduction:

If you live in a state with no income tax or have made significant purchases subject to sales tax, you can choose to deduct either state income tax or sales tax paid on your federal return.

Medical and Dental Expenses:

You may be eligible to deduct medical and dental expenses that exceed a certain percentage of your adjusted gross income (AGI). Keep track of out-of-pocket medical expenses, including prescription medications, health insurance premiums, and qualified medical treatments.

Educator Expenses:

If you are an eligible educator, you can deduct up to a certain amount for out-of-pocket expenses incurred for classroom supplies and professional development.

Student Loan Interest:

You can deduct the interest paid on qualified student loans, subject to certain income limits and other criteria.

Home Office Deduction:

If you use part of your home exclusively for business purposes, you may be eligible to claim a deduction for home office expenses, such as a portion of your rent or mortgage interest, utilities, and maintenance costs.

Job-related Expenses:

Certain job-related expenses that are not reimbursed by your employer may be deductible. These can include work-related travel, professional development, or job-specific equipment.

Keep Accurate and Detailed Records:

To substantiate your deductions and prevent potential issues during an audit, it is crucial to maintain accurate and detailed records. Keep receipts, invoices, bank statements, and other supporting documents related to your deductions. Organize them in a systematic manner to facilitate easy retrieval when preparing your tax return.

Time Your Deductible Expenses:

Timing your deductible expenses strategically can help maximize your tax savings. Consider the following strategies:

Bunching Deductions:

Bunching deductions involves timing your deductible expenses in a way that allows you to itemize deductions in one tax year while taking the standard deduction in another. By grouping deductible expenses into a single year, you may exceed the threshold for itemizing and maximize your tax savings.

Prepaying Deductible Expenses:

In certain situations, prepaying deductible expenses, such as mortgage interest or property taxes, before the end of the tax year can provide a tax advantage. However, it's important to consider the impact on your overall financial situation and consult with a tax professional before implementing this strategy.

Defer Income and Accelerate Deductions:

If you expect to be in a lower tax bracket in the following year, consider deferring income to that year while accelerating deductible expenses into the current year.

This strategy can help reduce your taxable income and increase your potential tax savings.

Maximize Retirement Contributions:

Contributing to retirement accounts can provide both long-term financial security and tax benefits. Take advantage of retirement accounts such as 401(k)s, Individual Retirement Accounts (IRAs), or Health Savings Accounts (HSAs) to maximize your tax deductions and potentially reduce your tax liability.

Consider Charitable Contributions:

Charitable contributions can provide significant tax deductions. Keep track of your donations to eligible charities, whether in cash or non-cash contributions, and ensure you have proper documentation to support your deductions. Additionally, explore the option of donating appreciated assets, such as stocks or real estate, to potentially maximize your deductions and avoid capital gains taxes.

Consult with a Tax Professional:

Tax laws and regulations can be complex, and maximizing deductions requires careful planning and consideration of your unique circumstances. Consulting with a tax professional can provide personalized guidance, help you identify additional deductions specific to your situation, and ensure compliance with tax laws.

Maximizing deductions is a fundamental strategy for optimizing your tax savings and reducing your tax liability. By understanding the difference between standard and itemized deductions, identifying commonly overlooked deductions, keeping accurate records, timing deductible expenses strategically, maximizing retirement contributions, considering charitable contributions, and seeking professional guidance, you can effectively maximize your deductions and optimize your tax situation. In the next chapter, we will explore strategies for handling self-employment income and expenses, providing insights into tax planning for self-employed individuals and freelancers.

UNLOCKING TAX CREDITS: TAKING ADVANTAGE OF AVAILABLE OPPORTUNITIES

Tax credits are powerful tools for reducing your tax liability and potentially increasing your tax refund. Unlike deductions that lower your taxable income, tax credits provide a direct reduction in the amount of tax owed. In this chapter, we will explore various tax credits available to individuals and businesses, providing insights into how to unlock these opportunities and maximize your tax savings.

Understanding Tax Credits:

Tax credits are incentives provided by the government to encourage specific behaviors or support certain activities. They directly reduce your tax liability, dollar-for-dollar, providing a more significant impact on your tax savings compared to deductions. It is crucial to understand the types of tax credits available and the eligibility criteria associated with each credit.

Common Individual Tax Credits:

Individual taxpayers have access to several tax credits that can significantly reduce their tax liability. Some commonly available individual tax credits include:

Child Tax Credit:

The Child Tax Credit provides a credit for each qualifying child under the age of 17. The credit amount is generally a fixed per-child amount, subject to income limitations. This credit can significantly reduce your tax liability, and in some cases, it is partially refundable.

Earned Income Tax Credit (EITC):

The Earned Income Tax Credit is designed to assist low-to-moderate-income individuals and families. The credit amount is based on earned income and family size, with higher credits available to those with qualifying children. It is a refundable credit, meaning you may receive a refund even if you have no tax liability.

Education Tax Credits:

Education-related tax credits include the American Opportunity Credit and the Lifetime Learning Credit. These credits can help offset qualified education expenses, such as tuition, fees, and course materials. Each credit has specific eligibility requirements and limitations, so it is essential to understand the details to maximize your benefits.

Savers Credit:

The Savers Credit is aimed at encouraging retirement savings for low-to-moderate-income individuals. It provides a credit based on contributions to qualified retirement accounts, such as IRAs or employer-sponsored retirement plans. The credit amount depends on your income and contribution levels.

Residential Energy Credits:

Residential energy credits are available for certain energy-efficient improvements made to your primary residence. These credits can help offset the costs of installing qualified energy-efficient equipment, such as solar panels, energy-efficient windows, or HVAC systems.

Business Tax Credits:

Businesses can also take advantage of various tax credits to reduce their tax liability. Some common business tax credits include:

Research and Development (R&D) Credit:

The R&D Credit rewards businesses that invest in qualified research and development activities. It provides a credit based on a percentage of qualified research expenses, such as wages, supplies, and contract research.

Small Business Health Care Tax Credit:

The Small Business Health Care Tax Credit is available to eligible small businesses that provide health insurance coverage to their employees. The credit can help offset a portion of the premiums paid by the business.

Work Opportunity Tax Credit (WOTC):

The WOTC is designed to incentivize employers to hire individuals from specific target groups facing employment challenges. The credit amount is based on a percentage of qualified wages paid to eligible employees.

Renewable Energy Credits:

Businesses that invest in renewable energy projects, such as solar, wind, or geothermal systems, may be eligible for renewable energy credits. These credits aim to encourage the use of clean energy sources and reduce reliance on fossil fuels.

Strategies to Maximize Tax Credits:

To maximize your tax credits and unlock available opportunities, consider the following strategies:

Understand Eligibility Criteria:

Thoroughly review the eligibility criteria for each tax credit to ensure you meet the requirements. Be aware of income limitations, filing status, and any specific conditions or documentation needed to claim the credit.

Keep Detailed Records:

Maintain accurate records and documentation related to the activities or expenses that qualify for the tax credits. This will help support your claims and ensure compliance with any substantiation requirements.

Explore Multiple Credits:

Understand that you may be eligible for multiple tax credits. Evaluate your situation to determine which credits provide the most significant tax savings and explore how they can be combined for maximum benefit.

Seek Professional Guidance:

Tax credits can be complex, and eligibility requirements may change over time. Consult with a tax professional or advisor to ensure you are aware of all available credits, understand the nuances, and optimize your tax planning strategies.

Stay Updated:

Keep abreast of changes in tax laws and regulations that may impact the availability or calculation of tax credits. Regularly review IRS publications, tax news sources, or consult with tax professionals to stay informed about changes that may affect your tax credits.

Tax credits provide valuable opportunities to reduce your tax liability and increase your tax savings. By understanding the types of tax credits available, meeting eligibility criteria, keeping accurate records, exploring multiple credits, seeking professional guidance, and staying updated on tax laws, you can unlock tax credits effectively. Maximizing your tax credits allows you to optimize your tax situation and keep more money in your pocket. In the next chapter, we will explore the unique considerations and strategies for handling self-employment income and expenses in tax preparation.

SELF-EMPLOYMENT TAXES: MANAGING INCOME AND EXPENSES EFFECTIVELY

Self-employment brings its own set of tax obligations and considerations. As a self-employed individual, you are responsible for managing your income, tracking expenses, and paying self-employment taxes. Understanding the intricacies of self-employment taxes is crucial to ensure compliance and optimize your tax situation. In this chapter, we will explore the key aspects of self-employment taxes, including managing income, tracking expenses, calculating self-employment tax, and strategies for effective tax management.

Understanding Self-Employment Tax:

Self-employment tax is the equivalent of Social Security and Medicare taxes that are paid by employees and employers. When you are self-employed, you are responsible for paying both the employer and employee portions of these taxes. Self-employment tax is calculated based on your net self-employment income.

Managing Self-Employment Income:

Managing self-employment income effectively is crucial for accurate tax reporting and minimizing tax liability. Consider the following strategies:

Separate Business and Personal Finances:

Maintain separate bank accounts and financial records for your business and personal expenses. This separation ensures clarity and makes it easier to track and report business income accurately.

Keep Detailed Records:

Maintain accurate and detailed records of your self-employment income. Track invoices, sales receipts, and any other documentation that reflects the income generated by your business.

Utilize Accounting Software:

Consider using accounting software to track your self-employment income. These tools can help automate financial record-keeping, generate reports, and simplify tax preparation.

Estimate Quarterly Taxes:

As a self-employed individual, you are required to make estimated quarterly tax payments throughout the year. Estimate your tax liability accurately to avoid underpayment penalties. Consult with a tax professional to determine the appropriate amount to pay each quarter.

Tracking Self-Employment Expenses:

Tracking and deducting eligible business expenses is essential for reducing your taxable self-employment income. Consider the following strategies:

Maintain Detailed Expense Records:

Keep meticulous records of all business expenses incurred. Save receipts, invoices, and bank statements that substantiate your expenses.

Categorize Expenses:

Categorize your expenses to make it easier to identify deductible business expenses. Common expense categories include office supplies, equipment, professional services, travel, advertising, and insurance.

Understand Eligible Deductions:

Familiarize yourself with the eligible deductions for self-employed individuals. Some common deductions include home office expenses, business-related travel expenses, health insurance premiums, and retirement contributions.

Consult with a Tax Professional:

Working with a tax professional can help ensure that you are accurately tracking and deducting eligible business expenses. They can provide guidance specific to your industry and help you maximize your deductions while staying compliant with tax laws.

Calculating Self-Employment Tax:

Calculating self-employment tax involves determining your net self-employment income and applying the appropriate tax rates. Here's a general overview of the process:

Calculate Net Self-Employment Income:

Start by calculating your net self-employment income, which is your total self-employment income minus allowable business expenses.

Determine Self-Employment Tax Rates:

The self-employment tax rates consist of the Social Security tax and the Medicare tax. These rates are subject to annual adjustments. As of the current tax year, the Social Security tax rate is 12.4% on the first portion of your self-employment income, up to a specified maximum amount. The Medicare tax rate is 2.9% on all self-employment income.

Calculate and Report Self-Employment Tax:

Multiply your net self-employment income by the appropriate self-employment tax rates to determine your self-employment tax liability. Report this liability on your tax return.

Strategies for Effective Self-Employment Tax Management:

To effectively manage self-employment taxes, consider the following strategies:

Retirement Contributions:

Maximize contributions to retirement accounts, such as Simplified Employee Pension (SEP) IRAs or Solo 401(k) plans. Contributions to these accounts reduce your taxable self-employment income while helping you save for retirement.

Health Savings Accounts (HSAs):

If eligible, consider contributing to an HSA. Contributions to an HSA are tax-deductible and can help offset medical expenses, reducing your taxable income.

Consider Entity Structure:

Depending on your business circumstances, it may be beneficial to consider the appropriate entity structure. Consulting with a tax professional can help you determine if forming an LLC, S Corporation, or other entity can provide tax advantages for your self-employment income.

Take Advantage of Deductions and Credits:

Ensure that you are taking full advantage of deductions and credits available to self-employed individuals. Examples include the home office deduction, self-employed health insurance deduction, and the Qualified Business Income Deduction (QBI).

Regularly Review and Adjust:

Regularly review your self-employment income, expenses, and estimated tax payments. Adjust your tax planning strategies as needed to align with your business's financial performance and changing tax laws.

Managing self-employment income and expenses effectively is essential for accurate tax reporting and minimizing tax liability. By understanding self-employment tax obligations, managing income and expenses diligently, calculating self-employment tax accurately, and implementing effective tax management strategies, you can navigate self-employment taxes successfully. Seek guidance from a tax professional to ensure compliance and optimize your tax situation. In the next chapter, we will explore strategies for dealing with tax audits and disputes, providing insights into handling these situations effectively.

RETIREMENT PLANNING AND TAX IMPLICATIONS: BUILDING A SOLID FUTURE

Retirement planning is a critical aspect of financial well-being, and understanding the tax implications of retirement accounts and strategies is essential for building a solid future. Proper retirement planning can help you save for retirement, take advantage of tax-advantaged accounts, and maximize your retirement income. In this chapter, we will explore retirement planning strategies and the tax implications associated with various retirement accounts and distributions.

Importance of Retirement Planning:

Retirement planning is crucial for achieving financial security during your retirement years. It involves setting retirement goals, determining the appropriate savings strategies, and understanding the tax implications of your retirement accounts and investments. A well-planned retirement can provide peace of mind and ensure a comfortable future.

Tax-Advantaged Retirement Accounts:

Tax-advantaged retirement accounts offer benefits such as tax deferral or tax-free growth, enabling you to save for retirement more efficiently. Here are some common types of tax-advantaged retirement accounts:

Traditional Individual Retirement Accounts (IRAs):

Contributions to Traditional IRAs may be tax-deductible, and earnings within the account grow tax-deferred. However, withdrawals in retirement are subject to income tax.

Roth IRAs:

Contributions to Roth IRAs are made with after-tax dollars, meaning they are not tax-deductible. However, qualified distributions from Roth IRAs are tax-free, including both contributions and earnings.

Employer-Sponsored Retirement Plans:

Employer-sponsored retirement plans, such as 401(k)s or 403(b)s, allow for pre-tax contributions, reducing your taxable income. Earnings grow tax-deferred, and withdrawals in retirement are taxed as ordinary income.

Simplified Employee Pension (SEP) IRAs:

SEP IRAs are designed for self-employed individuals and small business owners. Contributions to SEP IRAs are tax-deductible, and earnings grow tax-deferred until withdrawal.

Solo 401(k) Plans:

Solo 401(k) plans are available to self-employed individuals without employees. They offer similar benefits to traditional employer-sponsored 401(k) plans, including tax-deductible contributions and tax-deferred growth.

Contribution Limits and Catch-Up Contributions:

Each retirement account has contribution limits that dictate how much you can contribute each year. It is essential to be aware of these limits to make the most of your retirement savings. Additionally, individuals aged 50 and older may be eligible to make catch-up contributions, allowing for additional contributions above the standard limits.

Required Minimum Distributions (RMDs):

Most retirement accounts require individuals to start taking required minimum distributions (RMDs) once they reach a certain age, typically 72 years old. RMDs are the minimum amount you must withdraw from your retirement accounts each year. Failure to take RMDs can result in significant penalties. It is crucial to understand the RMD rules associated with each retirement account to avoid any compliance issues.

Roth Conversions and Backdoor Roth IRAs:

For individuals with high incomes, Roth conversions and backdoor Roth IRAs can provide tax advantages. A Roth conversion involves converting funds from a traditional IRA to a Roth IRA, potentially allowing for tax-free growth and distributions in the future. A backdoor Roth IRA involves contributing to a non-deductible traditional IRA and subsequently converting it to a Roth IRA.

Tax Strategies in Retirement:

During retirement, careful tax planning can help optimize your income and minimize your tax liability. Consider the following strategies:

Managing Taxable and Tax-Advantaged Accounts:
Carefully manage withdrawals from taxable and tax-advantaged retirement accounts to minimize your overall

tax liability. Balancing distributions from different account types can help optimize your tax situation.

Utilizing Capital Gains and Losses:

Evaluate your investment portfolio and consider harvesting capital gains and losses strategically. Capital gains can be taxed at lower rates, while capital losses can offset gains and potentially reduce your taxable income.

Timing Social Security Benefits:

Determine the optimal timing for claiming Social Security benefits. Delaying benefits can result in higher monthly payments and potentially lower taxable income if you have other sources of retirement income.

Charitable Contributions:

Consider making charitable contributions during retirement. Charitable deductions can help reduce your taxable income while supporting causes you care about.

Health Care Expenses:

Plan for health care expenses and understand the tax implications of medical deductions and health savings accounts (HSAs). HSAs offer tax advantages and can be used to cover qualified medical expenses tax-free.

Seek Professional Advice:

Retirement planning and tax implications can be complex, and individual circumstances vary. It is highly recommended to seek professional advice from financial advisors and tax professionals who specialize in retirement planning. They can provide personalized guidance, help you navigate tax laws, and develop strategies tailored to your specific goals and financial situation.

Retirement planning and understanding the tax implications of retirement accounts are crucial for building a solid future. By maximizing contributions to tax-advantaged retirement accounts, understanding RMDs, considering Roth conversions, implementing tax strategies in retirement, and seeking professional advice, you can optimize your retirement savings and minimize your tax liability. Take proactive steps today to secure a financially stable and fulfilling retirement. In the next chapter, we will delve into strategies for dealing with tax audits and disputes, providing insights on handling these situations effectively.

MAKING SENSE OF INVESTMENT INCOME: CAPITAL GAINS AND LOSSES

Investment income plays a significant role in building wealth and achieving financial goals. Understanding the tax implications of investment income, particularly capital gains and losses, is essential for maximizing returns and minimizing tax liability. In this chapter, we will explore capital gains and losses, their tax treatment, strategies for managing investment income, and the importance of tax-efficient investing.

Understanding Capital Gains and Losses:

Capital gains and losses refer to the profits or losses realized from the sale or disposition of capital assets, such as stocks, bonds, real estate, or mutual funds. Capital gains occur when the selling price exceeds the purchase price, while capital losses occur when the selling price is lower than the purchase price.

Types of Capital Gains:

There are two types of capital gains:

Short-Term Capital Gains:
Short-term capital gains result from the sale of assets held for one year or less. They are taxed at ordinary income tax rates, which are typically higher than long-term capital gains rates.

Long-Term Capital Gains:
Long-term capital gains result from the sale of assets held for more than one year. These gains are subject to lower tax rates, typically ranging from 0% to 20%, depending on the individual's taxable income and filing status.

Tax-Loss Harvesting:

Tax-loss harvesting is a strategy used to offset capital gains by selling investments that have experienced losses. By realizing losses, you can use them to offset gains and potentially reduce your taxable income. However, it's important to be aware of the IRS "wash sale" rule, which restricts the ability to claim a loss if you repurchase the same or a substantially identical asset within a short period of time.

Netting Capital Gains and Losses:

Netting capital gains and losses involves combining all your capital gains and losses for a given tax year to determine the overall net gain or loss. Netting allows you to offset capital gains with capital losses, reducing your taxable income.

Capital Loss Carryover:

If your capital losses exceed your capital gains in a given tax year, you can carry over the excess losses to future tax years. This allows you to offset future capital gains and potentially reduce your tax liability in subsequent years.

Tax-Efficient Investing:

Tax-efficient investing aims to minimize the tax impact of investment income and maximize after-tax returns. Here are some strategies for tax-efficient investing:

Utilize Tax-Advantaged Accounts:
Take full advantage of tax-advantaged accounts, such as IRAs, 401(k)s, or Health Savings Accounts (HSAs). Contributions to these accounts may offer tax deductions or tax-free growth, allowing investments to grow more efficiently.

Asset Location:

Consider the tax-efficiency of different types of investments and allocate them accordingly across your taxable and tax-advantaged accounts. Generally, tax-efficient investments, such as index funds or tax-managed funds, may be better suited for taxable accounts, while tax-inefficient investments, such as bonds or actively managed funds, may be more appropriate for tax-advantaged accounts.

Buy and Hold Strategy:

Holding investments for the long term can result in long-term capital gains tax rates, which are often more favorable than short-term rates. By adopting a buy and hold strategy, you may minimize the frequency of taxable events and reduce your overall tax liability.

Tax-Aware Rebalancing:

When rebalancing your portfolio, consider the tax implications of selling appreciated assets. Strategically rebalance by adding new funds or directing new contributions to rebalance your portfolio rather than selling appreciated assets.

Consider Tax-Efficient Funds:

Explore investment funds specifically designed to be tax-efficient, such as exchange-traded funds (ETFs) or index funds. These funds aim to minimize capital gains distributions, which can help reduce tax liabilities.

Seek Professional Advice:

Tax laws and investment strategies can be complex, and individual circumstances vary. Seeking advice from financial advisors and tax professionals is valuable for understanding the tax implications of your investments, developing tax-efficient strategies, and staying updated on changing tax laws and regulations.

Making sense of investment income, particularly capital gains and losses, is crucial for maximizing returns and minimizing tax liability. By understanding the types of capital gains, utilizing tax-loss harvesting, netting capital gains and losses, considering capital loss carryover, adopting tax-efficient investing strategies, and seeking professional advice, you can effectively manage your investment income and optimize your after-tax returns. Remember that tax considerations should be part of your overall investment strategy. In the next chapter, we will explore strategies for charitable giving and the associated tax benefits, providing insights into how you can make a positive impact while optimizing your tax situation.

DEDUCTING HOMEOWNERSHIP EXPENSES: MORTGAGE INTEREST, PROPERTY TAXES, AND MORE

Owning a home comes with various expenses, but it also offers potential tax benefits. Deducting homeownership expenses can help reduce your taxable income and increase your tax savings. In this chapter, we will explore the key deductions available to homeowners, including mortgage interest, property taxes, home office expenses, and more. Understanding these deductions and their requirements is crucial for optimizing your tax situation as a homeowner.

Mortgage Interest Deduction:

One of the most significant tax benefits of homeownership is the mortgage interest deduction. Here's what you need to know about this deduction:

Qualified Mortgage Interest:

To deduct mortgage interest, you must have a qualified mortgage on a qualified home. A qualified mortgage is a loan used to purchase, build, or improve your primary or secondary residence.

Deductible Mortgage Interest:

You can deduct the interest paid on your mortgage loan, subject to certain limits. This deduction applies to both your primary and secondary residences, up to a certain amount.

Home Equity Debt Interest:

Interest paid on home equity loans or lines of credit may also be deductible if the funds were used for home improvements or other qualified expenses. However, the Tax Cuts and Jobs Act (TCJA) implemented changes, limiting the deductibility of home equity debt interest in some cases.

Property Tax Deduction:

Homeowners can also deduct property taxes paid on their primary and secondary residences. Here are the key points to consider:

Deductible Property Taxes:

Property taxes assessed by state and local governments are generally deductible. You can deduct the amount paid for the year, subject to certain limits and restrictions.

The TCJA introduced a limitation on the deduction for state and local taxes (SALT), including property taxes. The deduction is now limited to $10,000 ($5,000 if married filing separately) for combined state and local income taxes, property taxes, and sales taxes.

Home Office Deduction:

If you use a portion of your home exclusively for business purposes, you may be eligible for the home office deduction. Here are some important considerations:

Qualifying for the Home Office Deduction:

To claim the home office deduction, the space must be used regularly and exclusively for business purposes. It should be your principal place of business or used for meeting clients or customers.

Methods for Calculating the Deduction:

You can use either the simplified method or the regular method to calculate your home office deduction. The simplified method allows a standard deduction based on the square footage of the office space, while the regular method involves tracking and allocating actual expenses.

Deductible Expenses:

Expenses that may be deductible under the home office deduction include a portion of your mortgage interest, property taxes, utilities, home insurance, and repairs or maintenance related to the office space.

Moving Expense Deduction (pre-TCJA):

Prior to the TCJA, homeowners who moved for job-related reasons could deduct qualified moving expenses. However, the TCJA suspended this deduction for most taxpayers, except for members of the armed forces.

Other Homeownership Expenses:

While not directly related to tax deductions, it's important to consider other homeownership expenses that can impact your overall financial situation:

Home Improvement Expenses:

Expenses related to home improvements or renovations, while not immediately deductible, can increase the basis of your home. This can be beneficial when calculating potential gains or losses upon the sale of the property.

Energy-Efficient Home Upgrades:

Certain energy-efficient home upgrades may qualify for tax credits, providing a direct reduction in your tax liability. Examples include solar panels, energy-efficient windows, and HVAC systems.

Mortgage Insurance Premiums:

If you have mortgage insurance, such as Private Mortgage Insurance (PMI), you may be eligible to deduct the premiums paid, subject to income limitations.

Documenting Homeownership Expenses:

To claim these deductions accurately, it's important to maintain detailed records and documentation related to your homeownership expenses. Keep track of mortgage statements, property tax bills, receipts for home improvements, and any other relevant documents that support your deductions.

Seek Professional Advice:

Navigating homeownership deductions and their associated tax rules can be complex. It's beneficial to consult with a tax professional or advisor who can guide you through the process, ensure compliance, and help you maximize your deductions.

Deducting homeownership expenses can provide valuable tax benefits, reducing your taxable income and increasing your tax savings. By understanding the deductions available for mortgage interest, property taxes, home office expenses, and more, you can optimize your tax situation as a homeowner. Keep accurate records, stay informed about changes in tax laws, and seek professional advice to ensure you maximize your deductions while staying compliant. In the next chapter, we will explore strategies for charitable giving and the associated tax benefits, providing insights into how you can make a positive impact while optimizing your tax situation.

EDUCATION EXPENSES AND TAX BENEFITS: NAVIGATING THE SYSTEM

Investing in education is a significant undertaking, but it can also come with financial benefits through tax deductions and credits. Understanding the tax implications of education expenses is essential for maximizing your tax savings and making informed decisions. In this chapter, we will explore the various tax benefits available for education expenses, including the Lifetime Learning Credit, the American Opportunity Credit, and the deduction for student loan interest. Navigating the tax system related to education expenses can help ease the financial burden and make education more accessible.

The Lifetime Learning Credit:

The Lifetime Learning Credit is a tax credit available to individuals who pursue higher education, including undergraduate, graduate, and professional degree courses. Here are some key points to consider:

Eligibility and Limitations:

To claim the Lifetime Learning Credit, you must meet certain eligibility criteria, such as being enrolled in an eligible educational institution. The credit is limited to a certain amount per taxpayer, based on qualified education expenses.

Qualified Education Expenses:

Qualified education expenses include tuition, fees, and any required course materials. However, expenses like room and board or transportation are generally not eligible.

Credit Amount and Phase-Out:

The Lifetime Learning Credit is non-refundable and can offset up to 20% of the first $10,000 of qualified education expenses per taxpayer. The credit gradually phases out for taxpayers with higher income levels.

The American Opportunity Credit:

The American Opportunity Credit is another tax credit available for higher education expenses. It provides more substantial tax benefits compared to the Lifetime Learning Credit, but with specific eligibility criteria:

Eligible Education Expenses:

The American Opportunity Credit covers tuition, fees, course materials, and required supplies. Similar to the Lifetime Learning Credit, expenses like room and board are generally not eligible.

Duration and Limitations:

The American Opportunity Credit can be claimed for the first four years of post-secondary education. The maximum credit amount is per student, per year, and the credit is partially refundable.

Modified Adjusted Gross Income (MAGI) Limitations:

The credit phases out for taxpayers with higher MAGI. It's important to understand the income limits to determine your eligibility for the American Opportunity Credit.

The Student Loan Interest Deduction:

The Student Loan Interest Deduction allows taxpayers to deduct the interest paid on qualifying student loans. Here's what you need to know:

Eligible Loans:

The deduction applies to interest paid on qualified student loans used for higher education expenses. Both federal and private student loans may qualify, but certain requirements must be met.

Income Limitations:

The Student Loan Interest Deduction is subject to income limitations. The amount of the deduction gradually phases out as income levels increase.

Deduction Amount:

Taxpayers can deduct up to a certain amount of student loan interest paid during the tax year. The deduction is taken as an adjustment to income, meaning you can claim it even if you do not itemize deductions.

Other Education-Related Tax Benefits:

Aside from the major tax credits and deductions mentioned above, there are other education-related tax benefits to consider:

Coverdell Education Savings Accounts (ESAs):

Coverdell ESAs are tax-advantaged accounts that allow you to save for education expenses. Contributions are not tax-deductible, but earnings grow tax-free, and withdrawals for qualified education expenses are also tax-free.

Section 529 Plans:

Section 529 plans are state-sponsored savings plans that offer tax advantages for education expenses. Contributions are not deductible, but earnings grow tax-free, and withdrawals for qualified education expenses are also tax-free.

Seeking Professional Guidance:

Navigating the tax benefits and requirements for education expenses can be complex. It's important to consult with a tax professional or advisor who can help you understand the available tax benefits, ensure compliance, and develop strategies to optimize your tax savings.

Understanding the tax benefits associated with education expenses is crucial for maximizing your tax savings and making informed decisions about pursuing higher education. By exploring the Lifetime Learning Credit, the American Opportunity Credit, the Student Loan Interest Deduction, and other education-related tax benefits, you can navigate the system effectively and reduce the financial burden of education. Be sure to keep accurate records of your education expenses and seek professional guidance to ensure you optimize your tax situation. In the next chapter, we will delve into the intricacies of tax planning for small businesses, providing insights into strategies for maximizing deductions and minimizing tax liability.

CHARITABLE CONTRIBUTIONS: MAXIMIZING TAX ADVANTAGES

Charitable giving not only allows you to support causes you care about but can also provide valuable tax benefits. Understanding the tax advantages of charitable contributions is essential for maximizing your tax savings while making a positive impact. In this chapter, we will explore strategies for maximizing the tax advantages of charitable contributions, including deductions for cash donations, non-cash donations, qualified charitable distributions from retirement accounts, and donor-advised funds. By navigating the tax landscape of charitable giving, you can optimize your tax situation while supporting organizations and causes that align with your values.

Cash Contributions:

Cash contributions to eligible charitable organizations are deductible on your tax return. Here are some key considerations for maximizing tax advantages with cash donations:

Eligible Charitable Organizations:
To claim a deduction, ensure that your donation is made to a qualified charitable organization recognized by the IRS.

Contributions to individuals, political organizations, and foreign organizations generally do not qualify.

Documentation Requirements:

To substantiate your cash donations, maintain records such as bank statements, receipts, or written acknowledgments from the charitable organization. Different documentation requirements apply depending on the amount of the contribution.

Deduction Limitations:

Deductions for cash contributions are subject to certain limitations based on your adjusted gross income (AGI). Understanding these limitations helps you determine the maximum deduction you can claim.

Bundling Donations:

Consider bundling multiple years' worth of charitable contributions into a single tax year to exceed the standard deduction threshold. This strategy, known as "bunching," can help you itemize deductions and maximize your tax benefits.

Non-Cash Contributions:

Contributions of non-cash items, such as clothing, household goods, or appreciated assets, can also provide tax advantages. Here's how to maximize tax benefits with non-cash donations:

Determining Fair Market Value (FMV):
For non-cash contributions, the deduction is generally based on the fair market value of the donated item. Properly valuing your non-cash donations is crucial to ensure accurate deductions.

Qualified Appraisals:
For substantial non-cash contributions, such as artwork or real estate, a qualified appraisal may be necessary to determine the FMV. The appraisal must meet specific requirements outlined by the IRS.

Qualified Conservation Contributions:
Contributions of qualified conservation easements or property for conservation purposes may provide enhanced tax benefits. Seek guidance from a tax professional or advisor knowledgeable in conservation contributions.

Recordkeeping:
Maintain detailed records and documentation for non-cash donations, including photographs, appraisals, and acknowledgments from the charitable organization. These

records are crucial to substantiate your deductions in case of an audit.

Qualified Charitable Distributions (QCDs) from Retirement Accounts:

Individuals aged 70½ or older can make Qualified Charitable Distributions (QCDs) directly from their traditional IRAs to eligible charitable organizations. Here's how QCDs can provide tax advantages:

Tax-Free Distributions:

QCDs are not included in your taxable income, allowing you to meet your required minimum distributions (RMDs) while reducing your taxable income.

Contribution Limits and Eligible Charities:

There is a limit on the amount that can be distributed as a QCD each year. Ensure that your donation is made to a qualified charitable organization to qualify for the tax-free treatment.

Donor-Advised Funds (DAFs):

Donor-Advised Funds (DAFs) are charitable giving accounts that allow you to contribute funds for charitable purposes. Consider the following when utilizing DAFs for maximizing tax advantages:

Immediate Tax Deduction:

Contributions to DAFs are tax-deductible in the year they are made, even if the funds are distributed to charitable organizations in future years.

Flexible Giving:

DAFs offer flexibility in timing charitable contributions. You can contribute to the DAF in one year and distribute funds to charitable organizations over several years, allowing for strategic tax planning.

Appreciated Assets:

Donating appreciated assets, such as stocks or mutual funds, to a DAF can provide additional tax benefits. You can avoid capital gains tax on the appreciation while still receiving a charitable deduction for the fair market value of the assets.

Seek Professional Advice:

Given the complexities surrounding charitable contributions and their tax implications, it's crucial to seek advice from a tax professional or advisor specializing in charitable giving. They can help you navigate the specific rules, maximize your tax advantages, and ensure compliance with IRS requirements.

Maximizing the tax advantages of charitable contributions allows you to support causes you believe in while optimizing your tax situation. By understanding the deductions for cash and non-cash contributions, utilizing qualified charitable distributions from retirement accounts, exploring donor-advised funds, and seeking professional advice, you can make a meaningful impact while maximizing your tax savings. Maintain proper documentation and records to substantiate your contributions, and stay informed about any changes in tax laws related to charitable giving. In the next chapter, we will delve into tax planning strategies for small businesses, providing insights into optimizing deductions and minimizing tax liability.

UNDERSTANDING TAX EXEMPTIONS AND DEPENDENTS: WHO CAN YOU CLAIM?

When preparing your tax return, understanding who you can claim as a dependent and the tax exemptions associated with dependents is crucial. Tax exemptions and dependents can significantly impact your tax liability and deductions. In this chapter, we will explore the rules and criteria for claiming tax exemptions and dependents, including qualifying children, qualifying relatives, the dependency exemption, and the Child Tax Credit. By understanding the guidelines, you can accurately determine who you can claim and maximize your tax benefits.

Qualifying Children:

To claim someone as a qualifying child, they must meet specific criteria outlined by the IRS. Here are the key points to consider:

Relationship:

The child must be your son, daughter, stepchild, foster child, brother, sister, half-sibling, or a descendant of any of these individuals. Adopted children and certain foster children also qualify.

Age:

The child must be under the age of 19 at the end of the tax year, or under 24 if they are a full-time student. There is no age limit if the child is permanently and totally disabled.

Residency:

The child must have lived with you for more than half of the tax year, except for temporary absences such as school or medical treatment.

Support:

The child must not have provided more than half of their own support during the tax year.

Dependent Exemption and Child Tax Credit:

By claiming a qualifying child, you may be eligible for the dependency exemption and the Child Tax Credit, which can provide significant tax savings.

Qualifying Relatives:

In addition to qualifying children, you may be able to claim certain relatives as dependents. Here are the criteria for claiming a qualifying relative:

Relationship and Residence:

The person must be related to you either by blood, marriage, or adoption. They do not have to live with you, but they must meet certain residency requirements.

Support:

You must provide more than half of the person's total support during the tax year. Support includes costs for housing, food, medical care, education, and other necessary expenses.

Gross Income:

The person's gross income must be below a certain threshold set by the IRS each year. The threshold amount may change, so it's important to stay updated on the latest guidelines.

Dependent Exemption:

By claiming a qualifying relative as a dependent, you may be eligible for the dependency exemption, which can help reduce your taxable income.

Dependency Exemption:

The dependency exemption is an amount you can deduct from your taxable income for each qualifying dependent you claim on your tax return. It reduces your overall tax liability. However, it's important to note that starting from the tax year 2018, the dependency exemption has been temporarily suspended under the Tax Cuts and Jobs Act (TCJA). Be aware of any future changes to tax laws that may reinstate or alter the dependency exemption.

Child Tax Credit:

The Child Tax Credit is a tax credit designed to help families with the cost of raising children. Here's what you need to know:

Eligibility:

To claim the Child Tax Credit, the child must be under 17 years old at the end of the tax year and meet the criteria for a qualifying child.

Credit Amount:

The Child Tax Credit provides a tax credit of up to a certain amount per child, depending on your income level. It is a non-refundable credit, meaning it can reduce your tax liability but cannot result in a refund.

Additional Child Tax Credit:

If the Child Tax Credit exceeds your tax liability, you may be eligible for the Additional Child Tax Credit, which is refundable.

Other Considerations:

Multiple Support Agreements:

In cases where multiple family members contribute to the support of a qualifying relative, a Multiple Support Agreement can be established to determine who can claim the dependent exemption.

Custodial and Noncustodial Parents:

In situations of divorced or separated parents, special rules apply to determine which parent can claim a child as a dependent. The custodial parent generally has the right to claim the child, but certain exceptions exist.

Education-Related Tax Benefits:

When claiming a dependent who is attending college or pursuing higher education, consider the education-related tax benefits available, such as the American Opportunity Credit or the Lifetime Learning Credit.

Seek Professional Advice:

Navigating the rules and guidelines for claiming tax exemptions and dependents can be complex. It's advisable to seek professional advice from a tax professional or advisor who can help you understand the specific requirements, optimize your tax benefits, and ensure compliance with IRS regulations.

Understanding who you can claim as a dependent and the tax exemptions associated with dependents is crucial for accurately preparing your tax return and maximizing your tax savings. By familiarizing yourself with the criteria for qualifying children and qualifying relatives, as well as the dependency exemption and the Child Tax Credit, you can make informed decisions and optimize your tax situation. Stay updated on any changes to tax laws related to exemptions and dependents and seek professional advice to ensure compliance and maximize your tax benefits. In the next chapter, we will delve into tax planning strategies for retirement and the associated tax advantages, providing insights into how you can optimize your retirement savings and minimize your tax liability.

INTERNATIONAL TAX CONSIDERATIONS: EXPATRIATES, FOREIGN INCOME, AND REPORTING

In an increasingly globalized world, individuals and businesses often face international tax considerations. Expatriates, individuals with foreign income, and those engaged in cross-border transactions must navigate complex tax rules and reporting requirements. In this chapter, we will explore international tax considerations, including taxation of foreign income, reporting obligations, tax treaties, foreign tax credits, and tax planning strategies for individuals with international ties. Understanding these key concepts is crucial for staying compliant with tax laws and optimizing your international tax situation.

Taxation of Foreign Income:

Worldwide Income vs. Territorial System:
Different countries employ either a worldwide income or territorial system for taxing income. Under a worldwide income system, residents are typically taxed on their global income, regardless of where it is earned. In contrast, a territorial system only taxes income earned within the country's borders.

U.S. Taxation of Foreign Income:

If you are a U.S. citizen or resident alien, you are generally subject to U.S. taxation on your worldwide income, regardless of where you reside. However, certain exclusions and deductions may apply to reduce the tax burden on foreign income.

Foreign Tax Credit:

To avoid double taxation, the U.S. allows a foreign tax credit (FTC) for taxes paid to a foreign country on foreign income. The FTC can offset U.S. tax liability on the same income.

Reporting Requirements:

Foreign Bank Account Reporting (FBAR):

U.S. persons with financial accounts in foreign countries may have FBAR filing obligations if the aggregate value of these accounts exceeds a certain threshold. The FBAR report must be filed annually with the Financial Crimes Enforcement Network (FinCEN).

Foreign Account Tax Compliance Act (FATCA):

FATCA requires foreign financial institutions to report information about U.S. account holders to the IRS. U.S. taxpayers with foreign financial assets above certain thresholds must also report them on Form 8938, Statement of Specified Foreign Financial Assets.

Form 8621 (Passive Foreign Investment Company):

If you have an interest in a passive foreign investment company (PFIC), such as certain foreign mutual funds, you may need to file Form 8621 to report and calculate the tax on the PFIC investment.

Form 5471 (Foreign Corporation):

If you are a U.S. person who owns or controls a certain percentage of a foreign corporation, you may have reporting obligations under Form 5471, including information about the corporation's operations and financial activities.

Form 8865 (Foreign Partnership):

U.S. persons who are partners in a foreign partnership may have to report their interest and other relevant information on Form 8865.

Tax Treaties:

Tax treaties are agreements between countries that aim to prevent double taxation and provide certain tax benefits to residents of the treaty countries. Understanding the provisions of relevant tax treaties can help individuals and businesses minimize their tax liabilities and comply with international tax obligations.

Tax Planning Strategies:

Entity Structure:
Choosing the right entity structure for your international business activities can have significant tax implications. Consider factors such as liability protection, ease of administration, and tax efficiency when determining the optimal structure.

Transfer Pricing:
For businesses engaged in cross-border transactions with related entities, transfer pricing rules come into play. These rules determine the pricing and allocation of income between related parties, ensuring that transactions are conducted at arm's length.

Tax Residency and Domicile:

Understanding the rules surrounding tax residency and domicile is crucial for determining your tax obligations in different countries. Consider the number of days spent in each country, ties to the country, and the presence of tax treaties.

Foreign Tax Credits and Deductions:

Maximizing the use of foreign tax credits and deductions can help reduce your overall tax liability. Ensure you properly document and claim any foreign taxes paid to avoid double taxation.

Seek Professional Advice:

Navigating international tax considerations requires expertise in both domestic and international tax laws. It is advisable to consult with a tax professional or advisor experienced in international taxation to ensure compliance, optimize tax savings, and effectively manage cross-border tax obligations.

Understanding international tax considerations is essential for individuals and businesses with international ties, including expatriates, those earning foreign income, and those engaged in cross-border transactions. By comprehending the taxation of foreign income, reporting requirements, tax treaties, foreign tax credits, and tax planning strategies, you can navigate the complexities of international taxation and optimize your tax situation. Stay informed about changes in international tax laws, seek professional advice, and ensure compliance with reporting obligations to avoid penalties and maximize your tax benefits. In the next chapter, we will explore tax planning strategies for estate and gift taxes, providing insights into how you can protect and transfer your wealth efficiently.

HANDLING TAX AUDITS: PREPARATION, RESPONSE, AND RESOLUTION

Receiving a notice of a tax audit can be a daunting experience. However, with proper preparation, a proactive response, and a thorough understanding of the audit process, you can navigate through the audit successfully. In this chapter, we will explore strategies for handling tax audits, including preparation steps, responding to audit requests, understanding your rights and responsibilities, and achieving a resolution. By familiarizing yourself with the audit process and adopting effective strategies, you can address the audit with confidence and ensure a fair and favorable outcome.

Preparing for a Tax Audit:

Review and Organize Records:

Gather and organize all relevant financial and tax documents, including income statements, expense records, receipts, and supporting documentation. Ensure that your records are accurate, complete, and well-organized to facilitate the audit process.

Understand the Audit Scope:

Carefully review the audit notice to understand the specific areas or tax years under examination. This will help you focus your preparation efforts and gather the necessary information for those specific aspects.

Consult with a Tax Professional:

Consider engaging a tax professional experienced in audit representation. They can provide valuable guidance, review your records, and help you understand the audit process and potential issues.

Conduct a Self-Review:

Perform a self-review of your tax returns to identify potential errors, inconsistencies, or areas that may trigger audit concerns. Address any identified issues proactively and gather supporting documentation to explain and support your positions.

Responding to Audit Requests:

Timely and Complete Response:

Respond to the audit notice within the specified timeframe. Provide requested documentation and information promptly and ensure that your responses are complete and accurate.

Maintain Open Communication:

Establish clear and open lines of communication with the auditor. Respond to their requests and inquiries promptly and professionally. If you require additional time or have concerns, communicate them respectfully and proactively.

Document Everything:

Keep a record of all communications and documents exchanged during the audit process. Maintain copies of letters, emails, and any other relevant correspondence to create a clear audit trail.

Seek Professional Representation:

Consider engaging a tax professional to represent you during the audit. They can serve as a liaison between you and the auditor, ensuring that your rights are protected and that you present your case in the most favorable manner.

Rights and Responsibilities:

Understand Your Rights:

Familiarize yourself with your rights as a taxpayer during the audit process. These rights include the right to professional and courteous treatment, the right to representation, the right to appeal, and the right to privacy and confidentiality.

Comply with Requests:

Cooperate with the auditor and provide the requested information and documentation to the best of your ability. However, be mindful of your rights and consult with a tax professional if you have concerns or need guidance.

Protect Confidential Information:

Ensure that confidential and sensitive information is appropriately safeguarded throughout the audit process. Limit access to documents and communicate securely when sharing sensitive information with the auditor.

Know Your Appeal Options:

If you disagree with the audit findings, familiarize yourself with the appeal process available to you. Understand the deadlines and requirements for filing an appeal and consider seeking professional advice to navigate this stage effectively.

Achieving Resolution:

Review the Audit Findings:
Carefully review the audit findings and explanations provided by the auditor. Seek clarification if needed and ensure that you understand the basis for any proposed adjustments or changes.

Present Your Case:
If you disagree with the audit findings, gather supporting documentation and present your case to the auditor or appeals officer. Clearly explain your position, provide evidence to support it, and articulate any relevant laws or regulations that support your position.

Negotiation and Settlement:
Engage in open and constructive dialogue with the auditor to explore potential resolutions. Negotiation may involve agreeing to certain adjustments, proposing alternative calculations, or reaching a settlement that is mutually acceptable.

Appeal if Necessary:
If you are unable to reach a satisfactory resolution during the audit, consider filing an appeal within the prescribed timeframe. Seek professional guidance to navigate the

appeal process effectively and present your case before the appropriate tax appeal authority.

Seek Professional Advice:

Handling a tax audit can be complex and stressful. It is advisable to seek professional advice from a tax professional experienced in audit representation. They can provide guidance throughout the audit process, ensure your rights are protected, and help you achieve a fair and favorable resolution.

Handling a tax audit requires preparation, proactive response, and a thorough understanding of the process. By preparing for the audit, responding to audit requests promptly and comprehensively, understanding your rights and responsibilities, and seeking professional advice, you can navigate through the audit successfully. Maintain open communication with the auditor, protect confidential information, and present your case clearly and substantively. If necessary, explore negotiation and appeal options to achieve a resolution that is fair and favorable. In the next chapter, we will delve into tax planning strategies for business entities, providing insights into optimizing deductions, credits, and overall tax efficiency for businesses.

RESOLVING TAX DISPUTES: APPEALS, TAX COURT, AND ALTERNATIVE OPTIONS

Tax disputes can arise between taxpayers and tax authorities due to disagreements on tax assessments, audits, or other tax-related matters. Resolving these disputes in a fair and timely manner is essential for maintaining taxpayer rights and ensuring proper application of tax laws. In this chapter, we will explore the various options for resolving tax disputes, including the appeals process, tax court litigation, and alternative dispute resolution methods. Understanding these avenues for resolution can help taxpayers navigate the complexities of tax disputes and achieve a satisfactory outcome.

The Appeals Process:

Requesting an Appeal:

If you disagree with a tax assessment, audit findings, or other determinations made by the tax authorities, you have the right to request an appeal. Follow the guidelines outlined by the tax authority for initiating the appeals process, including the prescribed timeframe for filing an appeal.

Appeals Officers and Mediation:

Appeals officers are impartial personnel who review the facts and applicable tax laws to facilitate resolution. They may propose settlement options, conduct settlement conferences, or engage in mediation to reach an agreement between the taxpayer and the tax authority.

Presentation of Your Case:

During the appeals process, present your case effectively and comprehensively. Gather supporting documentation, articulate your position, and provide evidence to support your claims. Consider engaging a tax professional experienced in the appeals process to strengthen your case.

Negotiating and Settling:

The appeals process provides an opportunity for negotiation and settlement. Engage in open and constructive dialogue with the appeals officer to explore potential resolutions. This may involve agreeing to certain adjustments, proposing alternative calculations, or reaching a mutually acceptable settlement.

Tax Court Litigation:

Tax Court Jurisdiction:

If the appeals process does not result in a satisfactory resolution, taxpayers can pursue litigation in the U.S. Tax

Court or other appropriate tax courts. Understand the jurisdictional requirements and filing deadlines for initiating a tax court case.

Representing Yourself or Engaging Counsel:
Taxpayers have the option to represent themselves in tax court cases, but it is highly advisable to engage the services of a tax attorney or other qualified tax professional. Tax court cases involve complex legal and procedural rules, and professional representation can help navigate these intricacies effectively.

Presenting Your Case in Tax Court:
Present your case in tax court by filing appropriate pleadings, gathering evidence, and preparing arguments that support your position. Adhere to the court's rules and procedures, and present your case in a clear and organized manner.

Appeals from Tax Court Decisions:
Both taxpayers and tax authorities have the right to appeal decisions rendered by the tax court. Understand the appellate process, including deadlines and requirements, if you choose to appeal a tax court decision.

Alternative Dispute Resolution (ADR):

Mediation and Arbitration:

ADR methods, such as mediation and arbitration, offer alternatives to traditional litigation. Mediation involves a neutral third party facilitating negotiations between the taxpayer and the tax authority, while arbitration involves a binding decision made by an arbitrator. Consider these options as alternatives to formal court proceedings.

Fast Track Settlement:

Fast Track Settlement is an ADR program offered by the IRS that expedites resolution for small businesses and self-employed individuals. It allows for the timely resolution of disputes without formal litigation.

Offer in Compromise:

An Offer in Compromise (OIC) is a settlement option for taxpayers who are unable to pay their tax liability in full. It involves negotiating with the tax authority to settle the debt for less than the full amount owed.

Collection Appeals Program:

The Collection Appeals Program (CAP) provides an avenue for taxpayers to resolve disputes related to collection activities, such as liens, levies, or seizures. It allows for an independent review of collection actions.

Seeking Professional Advice:

Resolving tax disputes can be complex and involve intricate legal and procedural aspects. It is highly recommended to seek professional advice from a tax attorney or qualified tax professional experienced in tax dispute resolution. They can provide guidance, representation, and ensure that your rights are protected throughout the process.

Resolving tax disputes requires a thorough understanding of the available options and strategic decision-making. By considering the appeals process, tax court litigation, and alternative dispute resolution methods, taxpayers can navigate tax disputes effectively and achieve a satisfactory resolution. Engage in the appeals process, present your case in tax court with professional representation if necessary, and explore alternative dispute resolution options when appropriate. Seek professional advice to ensure compliance with applicable laws and regulations and to protect your rights during the resolution process. In the final chapter, we will provide insights into tax planning strategies for individuals and businesses, highlighting key considerations for optimizing tax efficiency.

LEVERAGING TAX SOFTWARE: STREAMLINING YOUR PREPARATION PROCESS

Tax preparation can be a time-consuming and complex process, but leveraging tax software can significantly streamline and simplify the task. Tax software offers a range of features and tools that help individuals and businesses prepare their tax returns accurately and efficiently. In this chapter, we will explore the benefits of tax software, discuss key features to look for, and provide insights on how to leverage tax software effectively to streamline your tax preparation process.

Benefits of Tax Software:

Accuracy and Error Reduction:
Tax software is designed to perform complex calculations and apply the latest tax laws and regulations accurately. By automating calculations and eliminating manual data entry errors, tax software helps reduce the risk of mistakes on your tax return.

Time Savings:
Tax software streamlines the tax preparation process by automating repetitive tasks and providing guided

workflows. It eliminates the need for manual calculations, extensive paperwork, and manual form-filling, saving you valuable time.

Enhanced Efficiency:

Tax software organizes your tax information, imports data from previous years, and prompts you to provide necessary details. It helps you complete your tax return efficiently, ensuring you don't miss any critical information.

Access to Updated Tax Laws and Forms:

Tax software providers regularly update their software to reflect changes in tax laws and forms. This ensures that you have access to the most current tax rules and forms, minimizing the risk of non-compliance and maximizing your tax benefits.

Electronic Filing and Faster Refunds:

Most tax software allows for electronic filing, enabling you to submit your tax return electronically to the tax authorities. This speeds up the processing time and facilitates faster refunds, if applicable.

Key Features to Look for in Tax Software:

Easy-to-Use Interface:

Choose tax software with an intuitive and user-friendly interface. The software should provide clear instructions and guide you through the tax preparation process step by step.

Importing and Data Entry:

Look for software that allows you to import data from various sources, such as W-2 forms, 1099 forms, and previous tax returns. This feature saves time and ensures accurate data entry.

Calculation Accuracy:

Ensure that the software performs accurate calculations and supports various tax scenarios, including deductions, credits, and exemptions. It should update calculations based on the latest tax laws and regulations.

Error Checks and Review:

Choose software that performs error checks and reviews your tax return for potential mistakes or missing information. This feature helps identify errors or omissions before submitting your return.

Forms and Schedules Support:

Verify that the software supports all necessary tax forms and schedules relevant to your tax situation. It should provide the required forms for federal and state tax filing.

Access to Tax Resources and Support:

Consider software that provides access to tax resources, such as tax guides, FAQs, and customer support. This ensures you have assistance when you encounter tax-related questions or issues.

Leveraging Tax Software Effectively:

Gather and Organize Documentation:

Before using tax software, gather and organize all relevant tax documentation, such as income statements, expense records, and receipts. Having these documents readily available will make the data entry process smoother.

Follow Guided Workflows:

Tax software typically provides guided workflows that walk you through each section of your tax return. Follow these workflows to ensure you provide all necessary information and complete the return accurately.

Double-Check Inputted Data:

While tax software helps minimize errors, it's still important to review the data you enter. Double-check the information you input to ensure accuracy and completeness.

Utilize Data Importing:

Take advantage of data importing features to import information from previous tax returns, W-2 forms, and 1099 forms. This saves time and ensures consistency in your tax information.

Maximize Deduction and Credit Optimization Tools:

Explore the deduction and credit optimization tools within the tax software. These features help identify eligible deductions and credits, maximizing your tax savings.

Review and Finalize:

Once you have completed your tax return using the software, review it thoroughly before submitting. Pay attention to any error messages or suggestions provided by the software and make necessary corrections.

Seek Professional Advice:

While tax software is a valuable tool, it's important to note that it may not cover all complex tax situations or provide personalized tax advice. If you have unique or intricate tax circumstances, seek professional advice from a tax professional or advisor to ensure compliance and optimize your tax situation.

Leveraging tax software can greatly streamline your tax preparation process, offering accuracy, time savings, and enhanced efficiency. Look for tax software with user-friendly interfaces, data importing capabilities, error-checking features, and access to tax resources. Follow guided workflows, double-check inputted data, and utilize deduction and credit optimization tools. However, be aware that tax software may not address all complex tax situations, so seeking professional advice when needed is essential. By leveraging tax software effectively, you can simplify your tax preparation process and maximize your tax benefits. In the final chapter, we will provide valuable insights into tax planning strategies for individuals and businesses, enabling you to make informed decisions and optimize your tax efficiency.

ONLINE RESOURCES AND TOOLS: TAPPING INTO THE DIGITAL ADVANTAGE

In the digital age, individuals and businesses have access to a wide range of online resources and tools that can greatly enhance their tax-related activities. From tax research and educational materials to tax calculators and financial management platforms, leveraging online resources and tools can provide convenience, efficiency, and valuable insights. In this chapter, we will explore the benefits of utilizing online resources and tools for tax-related purposes, highlight key categories of online resources, and provide guidance on how to tap into the digital advantage effectively.

Benefits of Online Resources and Tools:

Convenience and Accessibility:
Online resources and tools are available 24/7, allowing you to access information and tools at your convenience. You can research tax topics, access forms and publications, and utilize tools from the comfort of your own home or office.

Real-Time Updates:
Online resources are often updated in real-time to reflect the latest tax laws, regulations, and updates. This ensures

that you have access to the most current information, reducing the risk of relying on outdated materials.

Cost Savings:
Many online resources and tools are available at little to no cost. Instead of purchasing books or attending expensive seminars, you can access valuable tax-related information and tools for free or at a fraction of the cost.

Efficiency and Time Savings:
Online tools streamline tax-related tasks, such as tax calculations, document management, and record keeping. These tools automate processes that would otherwise be time-consuming and error-prone, saving you valuable time and effort.

Knowledge and Education:
Online resources provide a wealth of educational materials, including articles, guides, tutorials, and webinars, that can help you deepen your understanding of tax concepts and stay informed about changes in tax laws.

Categories of Online Resources and Tools:

Tax Research and Educational Platforms:

Online platforms such as official government tax websites, tax research databases, and educational portals offer comprehensive information on tax laws, regulations, and guidance. These resources can assist with tax planning, compliance, and research.

Tax Calculators and Estimators:

Online tax calculators and estimators allow you to calculate your tax liability, estimate refunds, and plan for future tax obligations. These tools often consider various tax scenarios and help you make informed financial decisions.

Online Tax Filing Platforms:

E-filing platforms enable individuals and businesses to file their tax returns electronically. These platforms simplify the tax filing process, provide step-by-step guidance, and ensure accurate submissions.

Financial Management and Accounting Software:

Online financial management and accounting software help individuals and businesses track income and expenses, manage financial records, generate reports, and streamline tax-related tasks.

Document Management and Storage Solutions:

Online document management and storage solutions allow you to securely store and access important tax-related documents, receipts, and records. These platforms often offer features such as document organization, search capabilities, and backup options.

Tapping into the Digital Advantage:

Identify Trusted and Reliable Sources:

When utilizing online resources, ensure that you rely on trusted and reputable sources. Official government websites, recognized tax authorities, and established financial institutions are typically reliable sources of accurate and up-to-date information.

Stay Informed about Security and Privacy:

When using online tools and platforms, be mindful of security and privacy considerations. Use secure and reputable websites, protect your personal information, and follow best practices for online security.

Leverage User Reviews and Recommendations:

Before utilizing online resources or tools, consider reading user reviews and recommendations to gauge their usefulness and reliability. Feedback from other users can provide insights into the quality and effectiveness of the resources or tools.

Customize and Personalize:
Take advantage of online resources and tools that allow customization and personalization. Tailor the information and tools to your specific needs and circumstances, maximizing their value and relevance to your tax-related activities.

Combine Online and Professional Advice:
While online resources and tools are valuable, they may not address all unique or complex tax situations. When needed, seek professional advice from tax professionals or advisors to complement the information obtained online.

Seek Continuous Learning Opportunities:

The tax landscape is constantly evolving, and tax laws and regulations can change. Stay engaged in continuous learning opportunities by exploring new online resources, participating in webinars or online courses, and staying informed about industry updates.

Online resources and tools offer a wealth of benefits and opportunities for individuals and businesses in their tax-related activities. By leveraging these resources, you can access up-to-date information, streamline tasks, save time and costs, and enhance your tax knowledge. Identify trusted sources, stay informed about security and privacy considerations, and customize the resources and tools to your specific needs. Combine online resources with professional advice when necessary to address complex tax situations. Embrace the digital advantage and tap into the vast array of online resources and tools available to optimize your tax-related activities.

TAX PLANNING FOR THE FUTURE: STRATEGIES FOR LONG-TERM SUCCESS

Tax planning is not just about meeting current tax obligations; it also involves strategic thinking and preparation for the future. By implementing effective tax planning strategies, individuals and businesses can optimize their financial situation, minimize tax liabilities, and position themselves for long-term success. In this chapter, we will explore key considerations and strategies for tax planning with a focus on the future. From retirement planning to estate planning, we will provide insights and guidance on how to plan strategically to achieve long-term tax benefits.

Retirement Planning and Tax Efficiency:

Understand Retirement Accounts:
Familiarize yourself with different retirement accounts such as 401(k)s, IRAs, and Roth IRAs. Understand the tax advantages, contribution limits, and withdrawal rules associated with each account.

Maximize Contributions:
Contribute the maximum allowable amount to your retirement accounts each year. By doing so, you can benefit

from tax deductions, tax-deferred growth, or tax-free distributions in the case of Roth IRAs.

Consider Employer Matching Contributions:

Take advantage of employer matching contributions to your retirement accounts. This is essentially free money that can significantly boost your retirement savings and provide immediate tax benefits.

Roth Conversions:

Evaluate the potential benefits of converting traditional retirement account funds into a Roth IRA. While a conversion triggers immediate tax liability, it can provide tax-free withdrawals in retirement.

Manage Required Minimum Distributions (RMDs):

Understand the rules regarding required minimum distributions from retirement accounts after reaching a certain age. Develop a plan to manage RMDs to minimize tax implications and maximize your retirement savings.

Tax-Efficient Investment Strategies:

Capital Gains and Losses:

Understand the tax implications of capital gains and losses. Consider strategies such as tax-loss harvesting to offset gains and losses, thus minimizing your overall tax liability.

Asset Location:

Strategically allocate investments in taxable and tax-advantaged accounts to optimize tax efficiency. Place tax-efficient investments in taxable accounts and tax-inefficient investments in tax-advantaged accounts.

Dividend and Interest Income:

Be mindful of the tax implications of dividend and interest income. Consider investing in tax-efficient funds or tax-exempt bonds to minimize your tax burden.

Tax-Efficient Withdrawals:

When making withdrawals from investment accounts, develop a strategy that minimizes tax impact. Consider the order and timing of withdrawals to manage your tax bracket effectively.

Estate Planning and Wealth Transfer:

Understand Estate and Gift Tax Exemptions:
Familiarize yourself with the estate and gift tax exemptions and the current tax rates. Develop an estate plan that minimizes potential estate taxes and maximizes wealth transfer to your beneficiaries.

Utilize Lifetime Gifting:
Consider making annual gift tax-free transfers to your loved ones. By using the annual gift tax exclusion, you can transfer wealth while reducing your taxable estate.

Establish Trusts:
Explore the benefits of trusts in estate planning. Trusts can provide tax advantages, asset protection, and control over the distribution of your assets, while minimizing estate tax liability.

Charitable Giving:
Incorporate charitable giving into your estate plan. By donating to qualified charitable organizations, you can reduce your taxable estate while supporting causes you care about.

Seek Professional Guidance:

Estate planning can be complex, and tax laws surrounding wealth transfer are subject to change. Seek professional guidance from estate planning attorneys and tax advisors to ensure compliance and optimize your estate plan.

Regular Review and Adaptation:

Stay Informed about Tax Law Changes:

Keep abreast of changes in tax laws and regulations that may impact your tax planning strategies. Stay informed through reliable sources and seek professional advice when necessary.

Regularly Review and Update Your Plan:

Regularly review your tax planning strategies to ensure they align with your changing financial situation, goals, and tax laws. Update your plan as needed to optimize your long-term tax benefits.

Monitor Life Events:

Life events such as marriage, divorce, birth of a child, or significant changes in income can impact your tax situation. Monitor these events and adjust your tax planning strategies accordingly.

Seek Professional Advice:

Tax planning for the future requires a deep understanding of tax laws and regulations. Seek professional advice from tax professionals or financial advisors with expertise in tax planning to ensure the effectiveness and compliance of your strategies.

Tax planning for the future involves strategic thinking, careful consideration of retirement planning, tax-efficient investments, estate planning, and regular review of your tax strategies. By implementing these strategies, you can optimize your financial situation, minimize tax liabilities, and position yourself for long-term success. Maximize contributions to retirement accounts, strategically invest to minimize tax implications, develop an estate plan that minimizes taxes, and regularly review and adapt your plan to changing circumstances. Seek professional guidance to ensure compliance and make informed decisions. By incorporating these strategies, you can build a solid foundation for long-term tax success and financial well-being.

A LIFETIME OF TAX SUCCESS: CONTINUING YOUR TAX JOURNEY

Congratulations! You have now reached the final chapter of "Mastering Your Taxes: A Comprehensive Guide to Successful Tax Preparation." Throughout this book, we have covered a wide range of tax-related topics, empowering you with knowledge and strategies to navigate the complex world of tax preparation. As you conclude this comprehensive guide, it's important to remember that tax preparation is not a one-time event but an ongoing journey. In this final chapter, we will explore the importance of continued tax education, staying updated on tax laws, and cultivating good tax habits to ensure long-term tax success.

Embrace Lifelong Learning:

Stay Informed about Tax Laws:

Tax laws and regulations are subject to frequent changes. Make it a habit to stay informed about updates and amendments to tax laws that may impact your tax planning and preparation.

Read Tax Publications and Resources:

Continue to read tax publications, guides, and resources to enhance your tax knowledge. Stay engaged with reputable sources, official government publications, and professional tax organizations.

Attend Tax Seminars and Webinars:
Participate in tax seminars, workshops, and webinars to expand your understanding of complex tax topics. These events provide opportunities to learn from experts and stay up to date with the latest tax strategies and best practices.

Explore Continuing Education:
Consider pursuing formal continuing education in taxation. Enroll in courses or programs offered by reputable educational institutions or professional tax organizations to deepen your expertise.

Cultivate Good Tax Habits:

Maintain Organized Financial Records:
Continue to maintain well-organized financial records throughout the year. Develop a system that allows you to easily track income, expenses, and important tax-related documents.

Regularly Review and Update Your Tax Plan:
Schedule periodic reviews of your tax plan to ensure it aligns with your changing financial circumstances and goals.

Update your plan as needed to maximize tax efficiency and adapt to evolving tax laws.

Keep Track of Tax Deadlines:

Stay vigilant about tax deadlines to avoid late filings and penalties. Create reminders or utilize digital calendars to ensure you meet all tax-related obligations in a timely manner.

Monitor Changes in Personal and Financial Circumstances:

Changes in your personal or financial circumstances can have significant tax implications. Continuously monitor and evaluate these changes to make necessary adjustments to your tax strategies.

Seek Professional Assistance:

Engage Tax Professionals:

Consider engaging the services of tax professionals or advisors when needed. They can provide valuable guidance, ensure compliance with tax laws, and help you navigate complex tax situations.

Utilize Tax Software and Online Tools:

Continue leveraging tax software and online tools to streamline your tax preparation process. Stay updated with the latest features and enhancements to optimize your tax efficiency.

Collaborate with Financial Advisors:
Collaborate with financial advisors to integrate tax planning with your overall financial goals. Their expertise can help you make informed decisions that align tax efficiency with your broader financial objectives.

The Journey Continues:

Reflect on Your Tax Progress:
Take a moment to reflect on your tax journey. Celebrate the progress you have made in mastering your taxes and acknowledge the confidence and knowledge gained along the way.

Share Your Knowledge:
Consider sharing your tax knowledge and experiences with others. Help friends, family, or colleagues understand tax concepts and guide them in their own tax preparation journey.

Stay Committed to Tax Success:
Maintain your commitment to tax success by remaining proactive, informed, and engaged in your tax planning and

preparation efforts. Embrace the mindset of continuous improvement and lifelong learning.

As you conclude "Mastering Your Taxes: A Comprehensive Guide to Successful Tax Preparation," remember that tax preparation is an ongoing process. Embrace lifelong learning, stay informed about tax laws, and cultivate good tax habits to ensure long-term tax success. Continuously review and update your tax plan, seek professional assistance when needed, and leverage tax software and online tools to streamline your tax preparation process. Reflect on your progress, share your knowledge, and remain committed to tax success. By doing so, you will navigate the complex world of taxes with confidence, optimize your financial situation, and achieve your tax-related goals. Best of luck on your continued tax journey!